LITTLE RED RIDING HOOD

Modern Curriculum Press
BEGINNING
TO
READ
Series

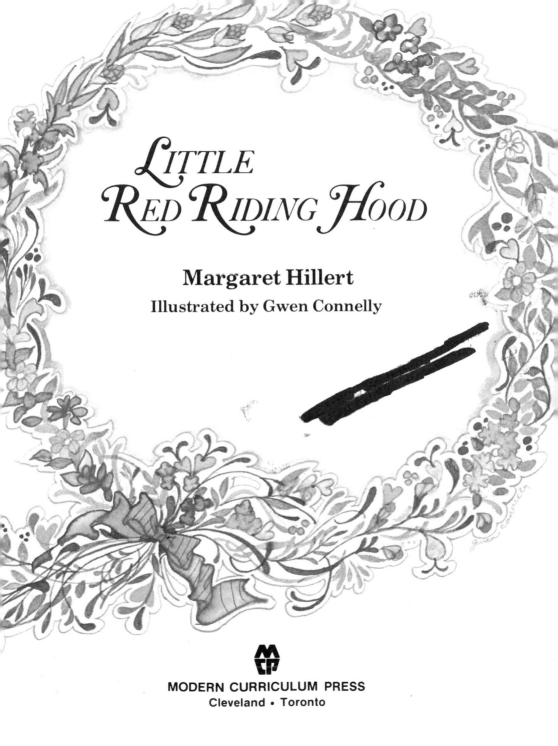

LITTLE
RED RIDING HOOD

Margaret Hillert

Illustrated by Gwen Connelly

MODERN CURRICULUM PRESS
Cleveland • Toronto

Library of Congress Cataloging in Publication Data

Hillert, Margaret.
  Little Red Riding Hood.

  (MCP beginning-to-read books)
  SUMMARY: Retells, in preprimer words, the tale of
the little girl who meets a wolf in the forest on her
way to visit her grandmother.
  [1. Fairy tales. 2. Folklore] I. Connelly, Gwen.
II. Title.
PZ8.H5425Li   398.2'1'0944 [E]   80–20983
ISBN 0-8136-5595-1 Paperback
ISBN 0-8136-5095-X Hardbound

3 4 5 6 7 8 9 10   88 87 86 85

Mother said, "Look here, little one.
Here is something for you.
Something red.
See how it looks on you."

6

The little girl said, "Oh, Mother.
How pretty it is!
I like it.
I like red."

7

"Now," said Mother,
"I want you to do something.
I want you to go to
Grandmother's house."

"Oh, good," said the girl.
"I like to do that.
   It is fun."

"Yes," said Mother.
"And here is something good
   to eat.
   Take it to Grandmother.
   Go on, now.
   Do not play on the way."
10

"No, Mother," said the girl.
"I will not play.
   I will run, run, run."

Oh, I like it here.
This is fun.
And I see something pretty.
Something pretty for Grandmother.

13

Red ones.

Yellow ones.

Blue ones.

I will get this and this

and this.

Oh, what do I see now?
Something big, big, big.
Do I like this big one?

"Yes. I am big,
but I like you.
I will walk with you.
What do you have?"

16

"I have something pretty
for my grandmother.
And I have something good
to eat."

"That is good.
You are a good girl,
but I have to go now.
I have to run."

19

And I have to run, too.
Where is Grandmother's house?
Oh, I see it.
That is it.

20

"Grandmother, Grandmother.
Here I am.
I have come to see you.
I have something for you."

"Come in. Come in.
Come here to me.
I want a good look at you."

"Oh, how did you get in here?
You look like Grandmother,
but you are not Grandmother.
Where is Grandmother?
Did you eat my grandmother?
I do not like you.
Help, help!"

"Here I come," said a man.
"I will help you.
See what I can do.
I can make this big one
run away."

"Get out. Get out,"
   said the man.
"Go away.
   We do not want you here."

"But where is Grandmother?
I do not see Grandmother.
Oh, I want my grandmother."

28

"Here I am, little one," said Grandmother.
"He did not eat me.
Come here to me.
My, how good it is to see you!"

31

Margaret Hillert, author of several books in the MCP Beginning-To-Read Series, is a writer, poet, and teacher.

Little Red Riding Hood uses the 69 words listed below.

a	get	make	take
am	girl	man	that
and	go	me	the
are	good	Mother	this
at	grandmother('s)	my	to
away			too
	have	no	
big	he	not	walk
blue	help	now	want
but	here		way
	house	oh	what
can	how	on	where
come		one(s)	will
	I	out	with
did	in		
do	is	play	yellow
	it	pretty	yes
eat			you
	like	red	
for	little	run	
fun	look(s)		
		said	
		see	
		something